MW01690344

UNDERGROUND

2014-15 NMI
MISSION EDUCATION RESOURCES

* * *

BOOKS

FOR WHOSE SAKE I HAVE LOST ALL THINGS
A Family's Story of Sacrifice
by Timothy R. Gaines

MIRACLE
The Power of Persistent Prayer
by Robert and Frances Collins

SONS AND DAUGHTERS OF BANGLADESH
by Elaine Bumstead

TO THE ENDS OF THE EARTH
Growing the Global Church
by Richard Gammill

THE UNSTOPPABLE CHURCH
Stories of Persecuted Christians around the World
By Spencer Baggott, Andrew Bennett, Dolphy Biswas, Timothy R. Eby, Dave and Rosie Kerr, Sylvia Potter, and Fletcher L. Tink

UNDERGROUND
Stories of the Persecuted Church in Africa
by Howie Shute

* * *

NEW ADULT MISSION EDUCATION CURRICULUM

Living Mission
The Unstoppable Church

UNDERGROUND

STORIES OF THE PERSECUTED CHURCH IN AFRICA

by Howie Shute

Nazarene Publishing House
Kansas City, Missouri

ISBN 978-0-8341-3201-6

Printed in the United States of America

Cover Design: Kelly Watts
Interior Design: Sharon Page

Names have been changed to protect the identities of the people involved.

10 9 8 7 6 5 4 3 2 1

CONTENTS

Dr. Howie Shute served as a Global Missionary in the Church of the Nazarene for fifteen years, serving as Field Director and Field Strategy Coordinator for the Horn of Africa and as Assistant to the Regional Director, responsible for church multiplication and development throughout the African continent. During his leadership, movements of God have taken place in a number of gospel-resistant African countries. Prior to Howie's call to Africa, he served eight years as a pastor and twelve years as a manufacturing executive.

In April 2012 Howie was honored with the Doctor of Divinity Degree by Africa Nazarene University in Nairobi, Kenya. In 1989 he graduated from Nazarene Theological Seminary in Kansas City, Missouri, where he earned the Master of Divinity Degree. Prior to his theological education he earned an engineering degree at Rochester Institute of Technology in 1974.

Howie is currently involved in mission throughout the United States. He serves with Holiness Legacy, promoting holiness summits across the United States and Canada. He speaks at revival services, holiness summits, and mission conventions, and holds missional strategy seminars for churches, zones, and districts.

1
THE INFALLIBLE PROMISE

"I will build my church . . ."
—Matthew 16:18

The week was a blur. So much had happened over the last twenty-four hours. We had left Bahir Dar at 4:00 A.M. the morning before. The dusty back roads were unending. Finding diesel fuel that day proved to be a challenge, but the Lord provided through some local people for a rather hefty price. It didn't seem like we would ever get to Metu, but we finally arrived at 5:00 P.M.

Ermias and I were teaching our new pastors in the area. The work of the Church of the Nazarene there was only about one year old, yet there were nearly a hundred new pastors to train. They were waiting for us and had been most of the day.

Just minutes after we arrived, I began the first teaching session. What a night. We poured our hearts out to these new pastors, teaching them what we Nazarenes believe. At first we were speaking to only our pastors, but many of the villagers had infiltrated our audience until there was no more room for anyone to sit. They wanted to worship, so we broke from our training and worshipped for two hours. We sang; we jumped; we danced. Then I preached holiness. These villagers had not heard that message yet.

It was now nearing 9:00 P.M. and we had much teaching yet to do. We dismissed the villagers, but they refused to leave. They wanted to worship, so we did until finally, at 11:00 P.M., we were able to send the worshippers home.

It was nearly 2:00 A.M. when we finished our first training conference in this predominantly Muslim area of the country. We had been going strong now for nearly twenty-four hours, and those twenty-four hours followed days of travel into and out of southeastern Ethiopia, where a new district had been organized in a highly Islamic area of the country.

It was no wonder that we found ourselves totally exhausted the next day. After a short night of sleep, we traveled the long gravel road that led to Mizan Teferi. We were expected at the district assembly there, as I was the assembly chairman that year. It was a challenge to keep our eyes open, although hour after hour the bumpy road worked to keep us awake.

And then, the unthinkable happened. Ermias, who was driving, fell asleep for just a moment, but that was all it took. I was in the passenger seat of the truck, and three of our pastors were asleep in the backseat. There was nothing anyone could do. The truck went into a spin as Ermias attempted to regain control, but the gravel under the tires fought against him. I can still see the high-tension electric pole rushing towards me. I was sure that we would not survive the headlong crash into it.

We hit the pole at such a high speed that it snapped in half, and we continued over the bank in a downward trajectory. We had left the road, and a steep ravine awaited us. We rolled over and over again, one way and then the other. My Ethiopian friends were all pleading with Jesus to save us. I knew the Lord would have to intervene if we were to live through this, since none of us were wearing seat belts.

As they cried out for our Savior's help, I thought, *How do I keep alive?*

I grabbed the handle above my door as we continued to roll. It seemed like an eternity as we toppled over and over for a distance of about two football fields. Then finally, the world came to a dead stop. And amazingly, we were still alive.

The roof had caved in on us and the doors were jammed shut. We crawled out the windows and found that we had come to a stop on the edge of a flat ledge, just short of toppling over the cliff into a raging river below. We couldn't believe it. Our bodies were sore, and one of our pastors had hit his nose in our jarring descent. There was blood gushing from his nostrils, but we were alive without serious injuries.

It took us an hour to reach the road again. The climb out was so steep that we had to hold on to the toppled saplings we had cut down in our tumbling descent. I needed a little extra help. As I pulled myself up the hill, one of our pastors pushed me up from below. On our way to the top, we noticed the Bibles, discipleship books, and tracts that were strewn all the way down the hill. We had filled the back of the truck with Christian literature to sell at the district assembly.

There were two villages near the crash site. Some villagers had heard the crash and the word quickly spread. Many came from their houses to see what had happened. They could not believe that there were survivors, and one exclaimed that we must serve a powerful God. The villagers began to climb down the hill and back up, again and again, to retrieve the literature that dotted the hillside.

As we organized the reclaimed literature into neat piles at the top of the hill, buses began to stop. Men and women climbed out to inspect the crash site.

Again, no one could believe that we had lived through the accident. We gave out Bibles and evangelistic tracts to the passengers and villagers who had gathered.

The district assembly was waiting, but the Lord had another plan. We never made it to Mizan Teferi that day, but many learned about our Savior. Our pastors returned to those villages over the days that followed and planted two new churches near our twisted, shattered, and abandoned truck. What Satan meant for our harm, God meant for good.

In Matthew 16:18, Jesus made a promise to his disciples. It was a promise for the first century, and it's a promise that still holds today. Jesus said, "I will build my church."

Who would have thought that Jesus would take a near-tragedy and use it to bring many into the kingdom of God? Who would have expected that Jesus would give us the opportunity to preach in the middle of the road to lost people who were passing by on buses, bound for other destinations? And who would have thought that the Lord would draw nearby villagers to an accident site just so they could hear about his amazing grace?

His promise will never fail. It is an infallible promise because it is a promise from God, not man. He will build his church. The church is unstoppable!

2

THE FALLIBLE ENEMY

"In fact, everyone who wants to live a godly life in Christ Jesus will be persecuted."
—2 Timothy 3:12

". . . and the gates of Hades will not overcome it."
—Matthew 16:18

It was a very dangerous decision. Omar was putting his life in serious jeopardy. Any Muslim would be risking his life making this same decision. In this country, abandoning Islam to become a Christian was simply impossible. And Omar was not just any Muslim. His family and his clan would not tolerate it.

Omar was the son of Ali, a well-known religious leader. Ali had memorized the entire Qur'an, which was a formidable challenge, given his poor skills in

Arabic. He was also a leading tribal elder. His passion for spreading Islam brought him the full support of the military government of his country. Ali was a most influential and notable leader in their homeland, and he wanted the same life for his son, Omar. He made sure that Omar received the best Islamic education possible, since Omar would succeed him as the religious leader in his clan. Little did Ali know that Omar was wrestling with the decision to become a follower of Jesus the Messiah.

Omar's journey to Christ began in the pursuit of his father's wishes. As Omar studied the Qur'an, he was impressed with the positive references to Jesus. Wanting to find out more about Jesus, he obtained a Bible so that he could more deeply study him and his teachings. Jesus began to impact Omar in ways he could not explain. He shared with his father his growing interest in Jesus Christ and questioned some of the claims of Islam. Ali was irate.

He lashed out at his son, "Omar, if you ever openly question the trustworthiness of Islam again, I will kill you."

Despite the threats to his life, Omar could not put the Bible down. Many passages spoke to Omar's heart, but it was the totality of Scripture and its authenticity that impacted him the most. For three years he resisted the Holy Spirit, delaying the decision to leave Islam and follow Jesus the Messiah. The decision, however, was constantly before him, begging his attention and his response.

The day finally came. The decision was made. The cost had been counted, but nothing could keep Omar from surrendering to Jesus. He confessed to the Lord his ignorance and his arrogance toward the Messiah and his Injeel.[1] Omar repented of his sins and began a new life with the Lord. However, Omar was very much alone, with no fellow Christians to guide him through this new life. But a Christian radio broadcast soon came to his rescue.

The broadcast personnel corresponded with Omar, answering many of his questions and providing the guidance he needed in his walk with the Lord. They sent him Bible study materials and discipled him from afar.

Omar was filled with joy as he testified, "The Bible assured me that all I needed to do to be saved was repent from my sins and accept Christ as my Savior—no more dogma or empty rituals, and no more constant fear of whether I will end up in hell or heaven."

It was a lonely walk with the Lord, but the broadcast became his source of spiritual growth and encouragement throughout his early days of following Jesus.

Omar yearned for his family to come to know his Savior. He first confided in his mother Afeefa about his new faith. As he talked with her about the Bible and Jesus, Afeefa's face grew red with anger.

"Omar, you are a rebellious son. Fear Allah; do not abandon Islam," she commanded.

As he shared his new faith with other family members and close relatives, he was branded as insane. He was threatened with every conceivable punishment if he did not recant his faith at once.

Omar persisted in his faith and pressed upon his family his argument for Jesus. He explained to them his reasoning for choosing Jesus, telling them that God did not send any prophet to abolish the Injeel of the Messiah. He told them that the Injeel was the final revelation of God and the Messiah Jesus Christ—the last messenger sent from God.

Omar was finally told to leave home. His family was sure that he would now become a pagan with a low and baseless lifestyle. He was thrown out. He was disowned, which was very painful for Omar. In his culture, identity and self-worth were derived from family, and now he was no longer Ali's and Afeefa's son. Omar had completely forfeited the acceptance and the protection of his clan. His inheritance was completely nullified. He was persona non grata in a country that would never accept his faith in Jesus the Messiah. It was only the grace of God that allowed him to hold onto his job in the midst of fierce persecution and trouble. And it was only the grace of

God that caused his family members to change their hearts, at least to some extent.

As a devout Muslim, Omar had always been well behaved and considerate. His good qualities increased now that he had become a Christian. His Muslim family and friends were surprised at the change in his life. They couldn't believe that the Messiah had made Omar a better person. He was allowed to return home, but because of his faith in Jesus, he was still not fully accepted.

For seven long years, his shortwave radio served as both his church and his pastor. He had not met one Christian during that time.

Then suddenly, everything began to change. He discovered that Ibraahim was also a Christian. He could not believe it. He had known Ibraahim but had not known about his faith in Christ. He was an underground Christian[2] just like Omar. Ibraahim and Omar, emboldened by their belief that there might be others who were secretly following Jesus, planted an underground house church in the capital city and pastored it together. In fewer than two years, the church grew to fourteen members. It was a wonderful blessing. Finally, the walk with the Lord was not so lonely. There were others to share the joys and challenges that came with following Christ in a radically Muslim country. But the new church would celebrate its second birthday in the midst of unprecedented persecution.

The security of the underground house church had been compromised. The Muslim officials discovered that there was a small but growing Christian community in their midst, and now the underground church faced persecution.

Ibraahim was the first Christian martyr. He was shot to death early one morning as he reported to work. Abdullah was next. He was shot and killed as he returned home from work one evening. His bullet-ridden body was found in the streets the next morning. Abukar was kidnapped and assassinated because of his faith.

The persecution continued. Dahkir and his wife Omera were sleeping in their bed when gunmen entered their home and killed them both while they slept. Their terrorized children ran from their home. Then it was Usman. He was riding home from work on a bus. When the bus came to a stop, men piled onto the vehicle and pulled him into the streets. They executed him publicly because he dared to follow Jesus.

Only two members of the underground church survived the carnage: Omar and another believer named Mahdi. Of the fourteen members of the church, twelve were martyred.[3] The murderers still roamed the streets of the capital city with impunity. The local authorities did not hold them responsible.

This small but vibrant church had been crushed. In a period of two years, all members but two were hunted down and executed wherever they were found. Mahdi went into hiding in his own country. Omar chose to flee to a neighboring country. After two years and several thwarted attempts on his life, Omar decided to escape to friendlier territory.

Satan gloated. The church was squashed. Twelve dead and one in hiding. Even Omar had run. This Islamic country was no longer at risk. So much for Jesus' promise that he would build his church and the gates of hell would not overcome it—at least, that would have been Satan's perspective. But there was more to the story.

As Omar fled into the neighboring country, he came into contact with the Church of the Nazarene and became a member. Soon afterward, he joined a Bible college and earned a bachelor of theology degree. During his four years of study, Omar planted a church in his newly adopted country.

The church was full of refugees from his home country. Omar began to make periodic trips back home to plant underground churches. In the first year, he planted one underground house church and trained the members to plant additional churches. By the second year, there were three churches in Omar's country. The third year it became nine; then the number grew to eighteen, and then twenty-five. Today, the Church of the Nazarene has more than one hundred underground churches in an overwhelmingly Muslim country. Despite the heavy persecution and martyrdom of many Nazarene Christians, the church is growing and becoming stronger. Additionally, Omar's younger brother has now accepted Jesus as his Savior.

Omar spent four years attending seminary in the United States and graduated with a master of divinity degree. While he attended seminary, he also planted underground churches in America, of all places. For even in America it is dangerous for a Muslim to become a Christian, especially if the news reaches his or her home country.

Today, Omar is serving as a global missionary for the Church of the Nazarene. His influence and ministry have resulted in house churches all over the world, even in nations that are closed to the gospel of Jesus Christ.

The persecutors of Omar's house church thought they had stopped Christianity from spreading in their country, but Jesus used their evil intent to further his kingdom there and elsewhere around the world.

In Matthew 16:18, Jesus made the promise that he would build his church, and he dared to say that nothing would stop him from accomplishing his purpose—not even hell itself. "I will build my church, and the gates of Hades will not overcome it."

Our enemy is not the Muslim people. The enemy of the church is Satan himself: "Your enemy the devil prowls around like a roaring lion looking for someone to devour."[4] Satan is waging a full-scale attack against the church. He is working at crushing the advance of the church, but no matter what the gates of hell thrust at us, nothing can stop Jesus from building the church. The enemy is fallible, but the promise of Jesus is infallible. While Satan is very much stoppable, the church is unstoppable!

3
DREAMS AND VISIONS

"I am the bread of life."
—John 6:35

Mohamed had never had a dream like this before. It was so clear, so real, so compelling. He just had to obey. He was sure the voice of God had spoken to him. He didn't know what his family would say if they found out. He had been warned about this many times. His mother and father had both instructed him to stay away from the Bible, and he had always obeyed them.

He knew that it was the book of the Christians, yet God had very specifically instructed him to find a Bible and study it. What could he do? He had to follow the will of God. It might have been a dream, but he somehow knew that God had used the dream to speak to him about searching for truth in the Christian Scriptures.

It wasn't an easy task to locate a Bible in his country. For anyone who was found with a Bible, life was as good as over. Even if you had not yet made a decision to turn away from the teachings of Islam, your Muslim family and friends would begin immediate persecution if they discovered you were reading the Bible. And if you failed to heed their warnings, you would be disowned. You would be thrown out of your family, excluded from your clan, cast out of your tribe, and maybe even killed for pursuing Christianity. Mohamed knew the risks involved, but how could he ignore the voice of God?

Where would he find a Bible? He couldn't ask anyone for help finding one. It was rare to find a Christian in his country, and even if he knew a Christian, it would not be safe to talk with him or her. Doing so was almost as dangerous as reading the Bible.

Mohamed thought, *If I am seen talking with a Christian, my family will think I am a Christian too.*

The next day, as Mohamed walked home from work, a man stopped him on the street. The stranger spoke to Mohamed as if he knew him.

"Read this," the stranger said. "It will change your life forever."

As the man walked on, Mohamed looked down at the object that had been placed in his hands. It was a Bible. Unbelievable! What a coincidence that this would happen at the same time he was looking for a Bible. Or was it a coincidence? In his dream the night before, the voice of God had told him to read the Bible. Could it have been God who placed it in his hands?

Once he began to read, Mohamed could not put the Bible down. He was mysteriously drawn to it every night. It was not easy to hide it from his family, though. He kept it under his mattress during the day, hoping his mother would not discover its hiding place. When he returned home each night after work, his mind was focused on one thing—that little black book hiding under his mattress. He could hardly wait to finish dinner and go to his room to read. It was unlike any book he had ever read before. It was so different from the Qur'an. There was such life in this book. And there was much on the teachings and life of Jesus.

The Qur'an always spoke well of Jesus, who was considered one of the prophets. The Bible, however, seemed to lift him above all prophets. Jesus himself declared, "I am the way and the truth and the life. No one comes to the Father except through me."[1]

The more he read, the more Mohamed began to fall in love with Jesus. He was especially moved when he read of Jesus' crucifixion. Islam had always taught him that Jesus had not been crucified. Muslim leaders scoffed and became angry at the idea that God would forsake one of his prophets. But Mohamed began to see that Jesus was God himself, who became a man to die for all men. Jesus willingly laid down his life so that his death would satisfy the great debt man owed God.

Mohamed could hardly believe it. *Jesus died for me. He died to take away my sins.*

What a revelation! He never would have guessed that eternal life was a gift from God. While reading the book of Ephesians, he began to understand that he did not have to work for his salvation. The Bible was quite clear on this: "For it is by grace you have been saved, through faith—and this is not from yourselves, it is the gift of God—not by works, so that no one can boast."[2]

Mohamed felt as though he would burst. The emotions that were building up in him begged for release. His heart was like a dam straining against a raging river, ready to overflow. Then he began to read through the Gospel of Mark. Jesus was in Galilee, preaching to the people and preparing to call his first disciples. His words jumped off the page, attacking Mohamed's mind: "The time has come. . . . The kingdom of God has come near. Repent and believe the good news!"[3] Mohamed fell to his knees and confessed his sins. In his heart, he knew that God had given him faith to believe that Jesus was God and had mercifully redeemed him.

What a rush. He had never felt like this before. He was as light as a feather blowing in the breeze. He knew his sins were forgiven. Joy and peace settled into his being.

Oh, the mercy of God, Mohamed thought, *to seek me out, call me in my dreams, put a Bible in my hands, and reveal the way of salvation to me—a sinner who had never sought him.*

Mohamed continued his study of the Bible, but he knew that he needed to find another believer with whom to share this new life. That was another challenge. How would he find another believer in this Islamic country? He began to pray, asking God for direction.

God's answer came again in a dream. This dream was very vivid, unlike most of his dreams. It was a crystal-clear picture in which he saw a country, the name of a city, and a church with two men inside it.

The voice came again. "Find these two people and seek further guidance from them."

When he awoke, he immediately made plans to leave home. His family was confused.

"Why, Mohamed, are you leaving your home?" his mother asked.

It was impossible to tell her that it was because of a dream, and even more impossible to tell her that

Jesus had told him to go. But in his heart, Mohamed knew that Jesus had spoken to him yet again. Jesus had shown him the country, the city, and the church he was to find. He had even shown him the two men with whom he was to speak. The country was right next door, a neighboring country with many Muslims, but there were also many Christians living there.

The trip was long and hard, but it was worth it. After reaching the city he had seen in his dreams, he spent the night in a local hotel. When he awoke the next morning, it was Sunday.

He had not been on the streets very long when he saw it—the church that had appeared in his dreams. When he stepped through the doors, his heart leapt within him. The people inside were singing joyfully. But it was not the songs or the joyful expressions of the people that made his heart leap. It was the two men leading worship. He had never met them before, but he recognized them just the same. They were the men from his dream, the men God had instructed him to consult for further guidance.

He could hardly wait for the worship service to end. When it was finished, he stood up, asking the pastor for permission to speak. He then told his story. He told of the first dream and the voice that instructed him to read the Bible. He told of the miracle God performed to put that Bible in his hands. He told of his study of the Scriptures and how he came to know Christ as his Savior. He shared with them how the voice of God had returned in his second dream, instructing him to find their church. Finally, he pointed to the two men.

He declared, “These are the two men I saw so clearly in my dream. These are the men from whom I am to receive further instructions.”

The church was amazed at his testimony and praised God for such a miraculous event. The two men then approached Mohamed and introduced themselves.

“My name is Ali. I am a global missionary with the Church of the Nazarene. And this is Ibrahim. He’s the pastor of this church.”

That morning a strong relationship began among Mohamed, Ali, and Ibrahim. Mohamed received not only instruction in the faith, but also strategic assistance as they taught him how to reach Muslims with an underground approach.

It was not long before Mohamed left for another country, fully equipped to reach Muslims wherever God might send him. And he had no doubt that further instructions would come. Mohamed knew that Jesus had become the Lord of his life and that Christ would continue to guide him in the days ahead.

* * *

Farah could not believe her eyes. Was it paint? Was it a permanent marker that had been used? Who would have done such a thing?

"Mother, come and look! Someone has written all over our wall in the living room," Farah cried.

Nagina rushed into the room to see what Farah was so upset about.

"Daughter," she exclaimed, "what in the world is wrong?"

Farah pointed at the writing she saw on their wall. Nagina stared at the wall in confusion. She could not see anything there, but Farah insisted.

"Right there! Look. Can't you see it?"

Nagina wondered if Farah was well. "Are you okay, Farah? Is something wrong?"

Farah persisted in saying that someone had written on the wall, but Nagina could not see a thing.

In exasperation Farah said, "It's right there. Someone has written, 'I am the Bread of Life.' What does that mean?"

Nagina was worried about Farah—she was obviously seeing things. But Farah didn't give up. When her brothers came home she led them to the wall, looking for someone to corroborate her story. But her brothers only laughed and dismissed the whole thing as one of those "female problems." She tried again that night when her father came home.

"Father, can't you see it? Tell me you do. Please tell me what this means."

This went on for days, and Farah became the laughingstock of her family and friends.

"She is seeing things," they said. Her family began to think she was going insane. But for Farah the words remained painted on the wall, haunting her day after day: "I am the Bread of Life." Finally, Farah herself believed that she was hallucinating.

One day, as she was visiting a nearby country, she met a pastor. He had stopped her on the street and witnessed to her about Jesus Christ. She would never dare to talk to a Christian in her home country, but since she was away from her family, she spoke with him.

Having become resigned to her "mental problem," Farah confessed to the pastor that she was seeing things that were not there. She told him the story of the words on the wall that only she could see. She did not know what they meant, but the message never changed.

"I can still see it there, written on our living room wall," Farah said. "'I am the Bread of Life.'"

The pastor smiled as he opened his Bible to John 6:35. Farah was shocked when the pastor showed her the same words written on that page. It was only a matter of days before Farah knelt down in the pastor's office, confessed her sins, and put her faith in

Christ. Jesus, who had spoken these words centuries before, had spoken them again to Farah.

* * *

Mohamed's and Farah's stories are not unique. While they live in communities unreached by the witness of Christians, the Lord has often intervened to bring people to Christ through dreams and visions. God is now orchestrating a massive movement among Muslims. According to an article by Kevin Greeson, one indication of this is "the increasing number of Muslims having dreams in which Jesus appears to them. The second most prevalent reason named by Muslims for why they came to Christ was dreams."[4] Greeson tells of a survey taken by Muslim Christians which indicated that 25 percent of them came to Christ in response to dreams.[5]

Nothing can stop Jesus from reaching people—even people who have been isolated from the gospel. It is a simple matter for God to overcome such barriers. Jesus can become real to anyone, even those who have not experienced the witness of Christians. Jesus can appear in dreams or visions to men and women who are lost and without hope. Nothing can stop Jesus from building his church. The church is unstoppable!

4

RULERS AND AUTHORITIES

"Pharaoh's heart was hard and he would not let the Israelites go. . . ."
—Exodus 9:35

Faisal, like most young men in the city where he lived, spent most of the day chewing chat. There wasn't anything else to do anyway. Finding employment was a daunting task. There were simply not enough jobs to go around. He was bored with school, and the streets seemed to provide all the diversion he needed.

At first it was great. Chat was the drug of choice for him and his friends. They chewed the narcotic leaf all day long, storing the residue in one side of the mouth until the cheek was stretched to the limit, while the juices produced an intoxicating effect.

What could be better? This little leaf brought the height of optimism. With a mouthful of chat, Faisal thought, *Everything is going to be okay. The day is approaching. Finally I will be a rich man. Significance is right around the corner. I will own the best house, have the most amazing wife, and be respected even by the elders of the community.*[1]

Yes, tomorrow it would all come together. And Faisal wanted these things. He needed to be important. He sought significance. He wanted a nice home and beautiful wife. Respect from his family and community would finally bring meaning to his life. Besides, he thought, this harmless little plant had to be good for you. It heightened his sensitivities so that his mind seemed to take on extra-sensory powers.

Chewing chat made him alert. And alert was good—at least until it was time to sleep. Then this heightened wakefulness became his enemy. If only his mind would slow down enough to catch a few hours of sleep. He had to sleep—his body was demanding it. Every night he lay there, pleading for the rest he so desperately needed.

Nothing worked. Nothing, that is, except for the mercy offered by the bottle next to his bed. Islam did not permit alcohol, or chat either, for that matter. Filling his belly with alcohol was the only thing that promised sleep. He would grab the bottle and drink, and drink, and drink, guzzling until unconsciousness reached out and took hold of him.

Mornings were not so good. If things had been depressing yesterday, waking and seeing that all his optimism was unwarranted made things bleaker than ever. To top it off, his stomach was sick, his head was pounding, and his whole body was screaming, *Get me out of here!*

There was only one thing to do. It was time to chew, and it all started over again—the promise of a brighter future, the sleepless night, the bottle of relief, and the disastrous morning, again and again. The cycle of daily drug-induced ecstasy and drunken stupors began to affect his brain. Little by little, Faisal began to slip from reality. Finally, his mind gave way and the streets became his home. Respect was gone, and the future promised only oblivion. No one talked to him. They wouldn't even look his way. Day after day, Faisal was treated like a dog wandering through his Muslim community.

But one day, a man bent down next to him in that dirty, dusty street and spoke a kind word. At first Faisal did not understand a thing the man was saying. He heard the name Jesus, but nothing made sense to him. For some time now he had been unable to understand even the simplest things.

And yet, there was something about the kindness in the man's voice and his message: "Jesus saves. He's more than a prophet—he's God himself. He loves you. He died for you to pay off your huge debt to God. Your sins are forgiven; just believe in him. Turn away from your sins. Turn to God. Walk with him."

Then the man reached down, lifted Faisal from the street, and embraced him. Faisal could not believe it. Here was a man who dared to embrace him. The stranger did not seem to mind that Faisal was dirty and drenched with body odors. Faisal could not remember when he had last showered or washed his face, yet this man really seemed to care about him. And the man's message was about Jesus, who cared for him more than anyone on earth.

Faisal soon noticed that there was something different about his mind. Things were becoming clear again. How could this be? What had rescued him from his mindless existence? Could it be Jesus? He listened more intently. It was a miracle. He really understood the man, and the message became clear. And right there in the depths of his despair, in the pit of his existence, in his dirty stinking clothes, Faisal made the decision. He dared to believe that Jesus is the Messiah. *He died for me,* Faisal realized. *I will walk with him.*

One cannot help but marvel at the change that takes place in a new believer. "If anyone is in Christ, the new creation has come: The old has gone, the new is here!"[2] And if that was true about anyone, surely it was true about Faisal. He had lived on the streets like a dog. He had lost his mind completely. He was known by everyone in the city as the dirty, mindless man. But now he had washed his body and groomed his hair. He spoke intelligently. Or did he?

He talked about Jesus to everyone who passed by. They knew about Jesus. After all, the Qur'an spoke of him as a prophet, and a most unique prophet at that. The Qur'an gave evidence of his virgin birth, his sinless life, and his ability to create out of nothing. The Qur'an even states that it will be Jesus who will judge the world on judgment day. Faisal, however, went far beyond the uniqueness of Jesus. He said that Jesus was God himself.

The people began to talk about Faisal. "That is blasphemous," they said. "There is only one God. Who could listen to this man, Faisal? He's still without a mind. He's insane for sure, but some are beginning to believe him. He's become a threat to our faith. Someone needs to silence him."

Faisal's country gave no room for Christianity, especially Christianity preached by a former Muslim. He had to die. An execution order was issued, and it was only a matter of time.

Faisal was walking down the street, looking for someone with whom he could share his Savior, when a policeman approached.

The officer cried out, "Christian?"

Faisal spoke with the anticipation of sharing Jesus. "Yes. I'm a Christian."

As the policeman approached, he reached for his pistol and aimed it precisely at Faisal's head. The bullet screamed from the chamber, down the short barrel, and point blank into Faisal's forehead. He crumpled to the ground, covered in blood.

Faisal lay on the street, apparently dead. But slowly, his head cleared and he regained consciousness. The bullet had miraculously ricocheted off the top of his forehead. He bled profusely because of the wound, but the bullet had not entered his skull. He rose to his feet as the policeman watched in disbelief. Faisal, expecting him to shoot again, decided he would not be shot in the back and die like a coward. He stepped toward the policeman.

The policeman froze, then turned and fled in fear, running from Faisal for all he was worth.

Faisal was also shocked. *I'm alive. How can it be? Jesus has saved me again!* he thought.

The word spread, and others began to plot Faisal's death. Faisal knew that the only way he could live to tell others about Jesus was to leave his country and retreat from his enemies so he would live to fight again. It was a fight to speak to his Muslim brothers and sisters about Jesus Christ, the Savior of the world.

Faisal made it across the border into friendlier territories. His adopted country would allow him freedom to express his newly discovered faith in Christ. At least, the government provided such freedom. It was still dangerous to share Christ with the Muslims of this country. Government approval was one thing, but permission of the community was another. For a Muslim to become a Christian completely shames the family, the clan, and the tribe. And Faisal needed another family. He moved to the capital city and found clan members there, but they would never accept his faith.

Then Faisal came into contact with a Nazarene Christian, and he began to attend a local Nazarene church. There, he grew closer to Christ and found a new family. He joined the Church of the Nazarene and became the first Nazarene from his country of origin, the first of his tribe. But his tribe would surely increase, because God had a plan for Faisal's life.

Faisal went on to lead many others from his home country and other Muslim countries throughout North Africa and the Middle East to Jesus Christ. The Nazarenes opened a radio studio in Faisal's new home city and asked Faisal to produce radio programs to broadcast back into his country of origin. Faisal was God's perfect answer for the new ministry. He had been discipled well in his local Nazarene church and was enrolled in a Bible college.

As his faith grew, so did his biblical understanding. He produced biblical programs that not only evangelized those in his home country, but offered strong discipleship teaching. Others from his home country came to Christ. Faisal communicated with them through e-mail and offered encouragement and training through his correspondence. Eventually, the radio ministry was expanded to reach the people of other Islamic countries in their native languages.

Later, Faisal became the coordinator of the radio ministry. In that role, he trained others to produce evangelistic programs and directed outreach to the Muslim world throughout the 10-40 Window.[3] E-mails and letters flowed into the church's secure post office box as Muslims around the world chose to follow Christ. People in countries completely closed to the gospel were hearing the truth about Jesus and receiving encouragement. Many found the radio to be their only source of discipleship. Faisal was right there, assisting in their spiritual development and helping them find underground churches near their villages.

Rulers and authorities of this world often stand against God and his kingdom. This is true throughout the world, especially in North Africa and the Middle East. Governments make laws that prohibit Christianity, and even if governments allow freedom of religion, communities often stand in the way. They stand against the church, God's holy people.

It was like that millennia ago when God sent Moses to deliver his people from the slavery of Egypt.

Pharaoh's heart was hardened against God's saving plan for his people. But God was not frustrated by Pharaoh's tyranny.[4] The rulers and authorities of this world can never frustrate God. God will raise up a Moses to lead his people out of Egypt; God will raise up a Faisal to reach Muslims across closed borders. He can raise a man from humble beginnings, even from the depths of despair. He can protect the life of a man, even when he is shot point blank in the head. God will always find a way to reach the unreachable. Nothing can stop Jesus from building his church, even when the rulers and authorities of this world stand against him. The church is unstoppable!

5

WILDFIRE

"Even the winds and the waves obey him."
—Matthew 8:27

The sun was scorching hot as Banak, Deng, and Tut made their way north on the Nile. It had been a long journey from Juba. Flies swarmed their exposed bodies during the day and mosquitos, showing no mercy whatsoever, attacked each night. They had little to eat on the way except for the dried maize they carried in their packs. Finding secure locations where they could safely spend the night was their biggest challenge. Travel in southern Sudan presented all kinds of challenges. Though the war between southern and northern Sudan had been put on hold, tribal warfare was always a problem. Nonetheless, the party of three pressed onward.

They had abandoned the boat they had chartered from Juba days earlier and were now on foot.

They were accustomed to walking long distances. Many times they had walked for days to take the Jesus Film to villages that could only be reached on foot. Last week they had carried the film equipment for five days so they could show the film to people living in a village without a church. Most of the equipment was light enough to carry without a problem, but the generator was a different story. Even when it was empty, it required two men to transport it. But today, as they pressed toward a village populated by animistic[1] people, it was filled with gasoline.

As Banak and Tut took turns shouldering the heavy generator, Banak said breathlessly, "Tut, did you know that they have now manufactured solar-powered equipment?"

"Solar?" Tut replied.

"Yes," said Banak, "you do not need a generator or gasoline or most of the equipment we are carrying. The sun provides the power for the sound system, the DVD player, and even the projector. The whole set of equipment is carried in one backpack."

Deng remarked that it would be his turn to carry when the solar equipment finally showed up in their district. Often the ministry team of three found others walking in their direction, and fellow travelers would gladly share their burden. The word usually reached the village where they were to show the film long before their arrival. A chattering crowd of people would join them before they reached the village, since many villagers had never seen a film before.

This time they targeted a village of 1,200 people. As they entered, children came running from every direction.

They chanted together, "Ma'ah lay!" This was the traditional greeting of the Nuer people of southern Sudan.

The women paused from their maize grinding and the men stopped their storytelling as they looked up to see Deng, Tut, and Banak enter their village with the crowd that swarmed around them.

As team leader, Deng immediately sought out the village chief. He needed to introduce his ministry team and gain permission to speak to the people. Deng explained their intentions thoroughly, and when the chief was finally satisfied, he nodded his head. Permission was granted.

The team quickly prepared the equipment while there was still light from the setting sun. Deng, Tut, and Banak had done this hundreds of times, and even with the children underfoot, they worked with great efficiency. The screen was secured and speakers were mounted on the screen poles. Cables ran from the speakers to the portable amplifier, and the projector was mounted on the table, along with the DVD player. Finally, the generator started and operated as they had hoped. That doesn't always happen. If not the generator, then sometimes the DVD player or video projector failed to cooperate. The technical problems had to be worked out before the sun moved below the horizon. The three men knew that sometimes equipment failure couldn't be explained by mechanical problems. Sometimes it seemed to be a spiritual matter, as though the equipment was demon possessed. At times they laid down their tools, knelt before the equipment, and prayed.

Today, everything worked as designed. Deng began to talk with microphone in hand, blasting the message across the village.

"Come and see a film. It is about Jesus. It will begin as soon as darkness creeps into the village."

The invitation was probably unnecessary. No one in the village would stay away on this night. When the film started, they were all there—all 1,200. The children sat on the ground, as close as they could get to the screen. Some of the adults sat behind them, but most stood and watched from that position. They were on both sides of the screen. That was how it worked: the film could be viewed from either side. Twelve hundred of them were focused on this very unusual event. For most of them, it was their very first film. A teenager climbed a small tree nearby. He had a box seat, maybe the best seat in the house, although not a very comfortable one. As they all locked their eyes on the screen, the film began to roll. It was the gospel story as told by Luke.

It didn't take long before Jesus became a hero for the villagers. The Nuer respect their elders because they possess wisdom, and Jesus spoke with such wisdom. His teachings were unique, and they admired his words. He spoke with such love. And what mercy he had! If someone was sick, he really seemed to care. Not only did he care; he also possessed the power to heal them. When the paralyzed man jumped to his feet and began to walk for the first time in his life, the villagers broke out in raucous cheers. One healing after another! In the film, many followed Jesus, but there was a group of people who seemed to hate him. He had enemies—that much was clear.

But when Jesus was nailed to the cross, the villagers cried out in disbelief. The children cried uncontrollably, and even the women joined in the mourning. The men cried out with anger. Someone almost threw a spear at the screen to stop the soldiers from killing Jesus.

As Jesus was lifted up on the cross, everyone gasped, and Deng paused the projector. The film went quiet as Jesus was suspended before their eyes. Deng began to explain that God came to earth in the person of Jesus Christ. He had come for this very purpose—to die. He had come to take humanity's penalty upon himself.

"All have sinned," Deng said, quoting Romans 3:23. "You have sinned. I have sinned. And because of our sin, we have been separated from God eternally.

"The Bible tells us in Romans 6:23 that 'the wages of sin is death.' That's our penalty for sinning—spiritual death, which is separation from God forever.

"But Jesus died for us. He took our death penalty away from us. All we need to do is confess our sins, turn away from those sins, and believe in our hearts that Jesus died for us."

Deng then invited the villagers to follow Christ. Sometimes the whole crowd would step forward, but tonight, only about one hundred came forward to confess their sins and turn to Christ. Tut liked it that way—he knew this crowd was really counting the cost and not taking the decision lightly.

After praying with the seekers, Deng asked them all to sit. There was more to come. He began the film again. The villagers watched as the soldiers took Jesus down from the cross and laid him in the tomb. The villagers stood there in silence, mourning the death of Christ. But then, they watched the women go to the tomb and find it empty. Before they knew it, he was standing there as big as day. Jesus was alive! All 1,200 of them began to shout and celebrate, even those who had not prayed earlier.

Deng explained, "God has raised Jesus from the dead. He's alive. And he's here tonight in our midst.

Since God has raised him from the dead, he is able to raise us from the dead."

Deng went on to explain that those who put their trust in Jesus will never die. He would raise them to new life to spend eternity with him in heaven. That night, the villagers returned to their homes with plenty to consider. They would never forget this night.

The next morning, those who had prayed the sinner's prayer the night before gathered under a tree. Deng had invited them to do so before he dismissed them the night before. They were all there—all one hundred new believers. They had gathered to begin a Bible study so they would understand more thoroughly the commitment they had made. They would receive instructions on how to follow Jesus. The class went as planned until one man in the group spoke up.

"Where will we worship each week? We don't have a building in which to meet."

Another said, "Let's construct a building now!"

And that is what they did. They were all experienced builders and had built their own homes. Sticks and mud (with a little manure added to make the mud dry with greater strength) were needed for the walls. Grass was used to make the thatched roofs. They each worked at different tasks. Some cut limbs from the trees, while others gathered mud or cut and piled grass. It took a lot of grass to thatch a roof, especially one as large as the new worship facility would have.

The church builders were not alone. It was the season for repairing roofs in the village. Every few years, new grass was gathered to re-thatch the roofs of the homes, and now, grass was piled everywhere in preparation for the thatching. Those building the church placed the cut grass in piles around the construction site, while others began building the walls.

They had been working on the project for several hours when some went to their homes to eat. One man had nothing at home, so he grabbed his AK-47[2] and went from the village in search for food. He came upon an impala grazing in the fields. Before the animal caught his scent, he squeezed the trigger, sending a bullet through its head. He dragged the impala back into the village and immediately built a fire.

While he was skinning and cleaning his game, a gust of wind blew sparks from his fire into one of the nearby piles of grass. The grass exploded into flames and the fire grew out of control, spreading from one pile of grass to another. The wind caused the flames to rage throughout the village. The fire consumed everything in its path as it approached the new Nazarene church. But then, the fire went out just as it approached the piles of grass that had been prepared by the new Nazarenes.

The villagers stood there dumbfounded. Their village had been destroyed. Many of their homes were gone. Only the new church had been spared. Who was this God that the Christians worshipped? How mighty and powerful was he? The villagers were so impressed that on the first Sunday the one hundred Nazarenes came together to worship, the rest of the people joined with them—all 1,200 villagers. They had come to worship the all-powerful God.

These villagers must have been reminded of the Jesus Film they had seen earlier that week. Jesus had been asleep in the boat as his disciples frantically tried to keep their boat afloat in the wind and waves that crashed against them. Just before their lives were lost, the disciples woke Jesus and cried out to him for help. Jesus stood and spoke to the wind and the waves, commanding them to be still. And the storm was over.

"Even the wind and the waves obey him!"[3] the disciples exclaimed.

Today, his disciples still see Jesus as sovereign over the universe. We often find ourselves at the mercy of the elements of nature. We have absolutely no control over these elements, whether they come as wind, waves, or fire. Jesus is always in control. He can stop the wind from blowing. He's able to still the waves. He can even speak to a wildfire and stop it in its tracks. Nothing can stop Jesus from building his church. The church is unstoppable!

6

MIRACLES

"Now a man who was lame from birth was being carried to the temple gate . . ."
—Acts 3:2

Rashid was highly respected in his village as a Muslim of great integrity. He loved people and always treated them as if they were his brothers and sisters. In fact, that is exactly how Rashid approached everyone—just as if they were his closest blood relatives. And people knew that Rashid really cared about them. He desired to be the best Muslim he could be. He read the Qur'an often and did his best to practice the five pillars of his faith. He would have liked to perform them in a more satisfactory way, but was prevented in doing so because of his problem.

Proclaiming the Shahada[1] was easy enough; all good Muslims recited the declaration of their faith in their daily prayers, as well as on other occasions.

He also joined his friends and family in fasting during Ramadan.[2] It was a small sacrifice to be made for his God. Zakat[3] presented a problem. How could he give alms to the poor? He was poor himself, and in his condition it was impossible to work. The Salat[4] presented even more difficulty. His desire to pray was not the difficulty; instead, his inability to perform the ritual of prayer made it impossible for him to speak to God. Moving through the required positions to make his prayer acceptable to God kept Rashid from performing Salat even once a day, to say nothing of five times a day. Prayer was an essential pillar of the Muslim faith, but he would never be able to bow with his hands on his knees, stand, prostrate himself on the ground, then sit in the special position. And he knew in his heart that he would never make the Hajj.[5] How could he ever get to Mecca? Even getting to the mosque in his village was challenging. Unless he was carried there by his friends, he would remain alone at his family's home.

Rashid was crippled. He had never walked, not once in his life. For more than forty years, Rashid had depended on his friends to carry him wherever he went.

One day, three of his friends hoisted Rashid to their shoulders and left his home with a specific mission in mind. Although their village was 90 percent Muslim, there were a few Christians who lived in their community. Rashid and his friends despised these Kafir.[6] They were nothing but infidels and unbelievers, the worst of pagans. A new church had been started in their village recently, and this church appeared to be more dangerous than the others in their community. These people were more vocal about their faith, and they were telling everyone about Jesus.

Rashid and his friends had nothing against Jesus himself. He was, after all, one of the prophets, and well-respected by all Muslims. But the Christians had gone too far. They preached that Jesus was more than a prophet. They made Jesus their God, and that was blasphemy. All Muslims believed that there was only one God, as they proclaimed every day in their prayers. But this new church was boldly preaching that there was great power available when you pray in the name of Jesus.

"God can do anything," they would say, "when you approach God in Jesus' name."

This, in fact, was the mission of Rashid and his friends on this day. They were going to embarrass the new church before the whole community. Rashid's friends couldn't help but smile as they carried him down the path to where the church had gathered for an outdoor service. This, they thought, would put the Christians in their place once and for all. They could hear themselves, even now, laughing at the infidels as they made excuses for their inability to heal Rashid.

When they arrived, they were surprised to see so many people gathered on the hillside, worshipping in the fields. There must have been 1,000 people listening to the pastor as he preached. There were hardly that many people living in the village. This new church had been growing in their region, and Nazarenes had come from surrounding villages to be here this day. That's what they called themselves—Nazarenes. There were probably 700 Nazarenes present, along with about 200 Christians from other denominations. Rashid and his friends recognized many of their Muslim friends who had gathered to observe the service. Their friends were also unhappy about this new church preaching in their village. There were about 100 Muslims standing at the back of the crowd of 1,000 people. The Christians were a little concerned about the Muslims behind them, unsure if the plan was one of protest or violence.

The pastor was preaching when Rashid's friends carried him into the service, but he stopped when the friends deposited Rashid right at his feet. The pastor knew Rashid. Who didn't? He was well known throughout the village as well as in the surrounding communities. He was respected because of his good life, but he was best known for being crippled from birth. Almost everyone there knew Rashid and his story. As the pastor stopped preaching, he looked into the smirking faces of Rashid's friends.

"Why have you brought him here today? Why have you interrupted our worship by laying Rashid before me?" asked the pastor.

The three men responded that they brought Rashid to the church for healing. The pastor recognized the challenge that was put before the church that day. Even more, he understood that Jesus himself was being challenged.

The pastor exclaimed, "I have no magic in my hands!" to distance himself from the many witch doctors who practiced in that area. "In fact, I have no power or ability to heal this man and make him walk. But this Jesus I have been preaching about has the power. He has the ability. I do not know what his will is, but let's pray and see what Jesus might do."

The pastor knelt by Rashid, placed his hands on him, and began to pray. The people in the front of the crowd first saw that something was happening. As the pastor prayed, Rashid's twisted legs began to straighten and thicken as he gained strength in his limbs for the first time. Those in the front gasped as they saw with their own eyes that God had performed a miracle for this crippled man. Rashid himself sensed God working in his legs. He felt at first a tingling sensation, then a movement of the muscles in his useless legs. Rashid began to stand, very carefully at first. Then, courage came from somewhere—where, he didn't know. He pushed himself up with his hands and wobbled before the crowd. One step led to another, and he began to realize that he was on his feet, walking first to the left, then to the right. Walking became skipping, and skipping broke into a dance.

"Praise God!" he cried out. "I can walk!"

The crowd came to life. They could not believe their eyes. Rashid was walking and dancing. He was on his feet for the first time in his life. He had spent forty years being carried by his friends, but today, he would walk home on his own. They could not help it. They began to shout and sing and praise God. They joined Rashid in his dance of joy. A thousand people danced before the Lord, celebrating this miracle of God. Well, almost 1,000.

The Muslims in the back of the crowd were visibly moved, even agitated. Then forty of them came rushing through the crowd. They pushed and shoved their way to the front, their eyes focused on the pastor. When they broke through the front of the crowd, they rushed to the man who had prayed in the name of Jesus.

As they came close to him, they dropped to their knees and cried out, "Pastor, pray for us. We need Jesus."

Forty Muslims came to Christ that day. Many more would come to Christ in that village and in the surrounding communities in the days that followed. But on that day, forty courageous souls put their lives on the line as they publicly prayed, confessing their sins and putting their trust in Jesus as Savior.

Muslims cannot leave Islam and become Christians without severe persecution. It is a shame for the family, the clan, and even the tribe for such a thing to happen to one of their own. Their son or their daughter, or their brother or their sister becomes an infidel, bringing disgrace to all of Islam. Muslims who forsake Islam to become Christians know very well that they will be disowned by their community and disinherited by their family. They know that someone may even kill them to remove the shame they have brought upon the faith. Muslims count the cost. They know what a decision for Christ will bring them. And yet today, Muslims are coming to Christ in unprecedented numbers, many of them in response to miracles just like the one that gave Rashid his new legs.

Miracles are not a new phenomenon in the church. Jesus performed many miracles in his three years of ministry, and his disciples continued his ministry of miracles by praying in his name. In one such instance, Peter and John were going to the temple at the time of prayer.[7] On their way, they met a crippled man who had been laid on the steps of the temple to beg from all those coming to pray. This man was so much like Rashid. He had been carried to the temple, was crippled from birth, and was over forty years of age. He also had come to the house of God with ulterior motives. Peter and John did not respond to his begging as he had hoped. They gave him no money, but what he received was much better than his expectation. Instead, in the name of Jesus, Peter and John spoke to the crippled man and he rose to his feet, able to walk for the first time.

Jesus used these miracles to draw people to himself, and today, the Lord sometimes still uses miracles to reach those so far from him. Jesus performs miracles to fight against the enemy, who has enslaved so many. Yes, the church is truly unstoppable.

7
DEMONS

"The demons begged Jesus, 'Send us among the pigs.' . . . He gave them permission."
—Mark 5:12-13

Safia was on the run. She had fled her home country because of severe persecution. Three others from her underground house church were with her when I first met her. We had arranged a safe house for them to live in for the next three months. After that, they would go back to their home country, although they would return to a different city than the one from which they had fled. By then, their pursuers would have given up their search. At least we hoped so.

They had been worshipping in the homes of their members for more than a year without being noticed by the community. They had felt safe there and were overjoyed to assemble each Friday and worship together. To fellowship with other Christians was a privilege they never took for granted.

Living in such a strongly Islamic country presented great challenges to living out their faith in Christ. They actively shared their faith in their community, but this could be done only through careful, private encounters with those they had come to trust. Building strong relationships was critical before they began to witness. The process took time and a great deal of wisdom, but the Lord provided many opportunities for them to discuss Jesus with others. Their Muslim friends were slowly but surely coming to Christ.

After coming to Christ, their friends would join them in worship in their small but growing house church. Sometimes individuals who were seeking Jesus but had not yet made the decision to leave Islam would join them in their Friday meetings. Allowing such people to join came with a risk. It took a unanimous decision by the group members before they were invited to the worship gatherings. That was also true for those who professed a conversion experience. One never knew for sure whether the new person was sincere about their commitment to Jesus or was a plant to infiltrate the group. If their meetings were reported, everyone in the church would be in danger, and that church could be extinguished by an attack upon the members.

So far, their church had been very successful in the screening process. All of their church members were sincere followers of Christ, or at least genuine seekers of Jesus. Safia was one of those seekers, and she had a problem. She did not completely understand it, but it had been wreaking havoc in her life. She was hoping that somehow Jesus might help her with this problem.

Some foreigners had arrived in her city. They were Christians, and they were public about their worship. Since the foreigners were not of Muslim background, the community would overlook their meetings as long as they kept to themselves. But they did not keep their faith to themselves. They opened their windows and sang and preached loudly so that those who could hear might decide to join them. It was not long before the police arrived and arrested all the Christians for disturbing the community with their evangelistic advances.

One of Safia's house church members went to visit these people in jail. Visiting those in prison was a compassionate thing to do, but it was not safe. A policeman became suspicious of the visitor. Who in their country would visit a foreigner in prison, and a Christian foreigner at that? The policeman decided to follow the man, and he watched him carefully for a number of days. He was still observing the man's activities when Friday came. He followed the man to the home where Safia's church had been meeting.

The policeman knew right away that this was some kind of a secret meeting, and he soon discovered that it was a group of Christians. It was a house full of infidels, unbelievers, and blasphemers of Islam. It wasn't long before he discovered the name of each person who had attended the meetings. The first to be arrested was the pastor. Then others were dragged from their homes and taken to jail. No one knew what would become of their fellow church members. More and more were arrested. It was then that Safia and her three friends decided to run until they reached our city of refuge where the Church of the Nazarene had rented a safe house. It would be their home until things quieted down in their home country.

A week after they arrived, one of our leaders came to me.

"Howie," he said, "we have a problem at the safe house."

He explained that the landlord was ready to kick our four refugees out of his house because the neighbors had been complaining. Every night the neighbors were disturbed by one of the refugee women who would cry out during the night, screaming and crying and moaning. They would not put up with it any longer.

Our leader finally told me, "I think Safia is demon possessed. Can you come and pray for her with us?"

We left immediately. I went to the safe house, accompanied by three of our leaders who were from the same tribal background as Safia. We met Safia's three friends when we arrived at the home, and their faces gave away their exasperation and confusion. They did not know what to do for Safia. She was normal much of the time, but in the evenings she would go into a trance-like state. She would cry out in great pain, hold her stomach, and roll on the ground in agony. She was in this terrifying state even as we walked in the door.

Our leaders had briefed me that Safia came from an Islamic family that had allowed traditional beliefs to permeate their Islamic faith. In fact, Safia's mother was a witch doctor, as her grandmother had been. The practice went back as far as the family could remember. Safia was expected to follow in the footsteps of the women before her; that was her problem. The family tradition wrecked her life as the demonic spirit that passed through her family from generation to generation took up residence in her body. Ashamed, she had kept this secret from the church. She wanted nothing to do with the demon, but the demon would not let her go.[1]

We walked into Safia's bedroom. She was on the floor on her mattress, obviously in pain. She was moaning with eyes closed. I moved to Safia and laid my hands on her head. The others joined in prayer with me. We pleaded with the Lord to set her free. As we commanded the demon to leave her in the name of Jesus, her body grew quiet.

I instructed her, "Safia, say 'Jesus is Lord.'"

At first she just lay there, unresponsive. I spoke to her again and again.

"Say it, Safia! Proclaim aloud, 'Jesus is Lord.'"

Finally, she began to speak.

"Jesus is . . ." But before she could finish this statement of faith, she grabbed her stomach and cried out in pain. Her body rolled and shook as we continued to pray.

"In the name of Jesus we command you, evil spirit, to leave Safia at once."

I can't tell you how many times we commanded the demon to leave her. Eventually, her body would become still again. We would repeat the instructions.

"Safia, say it! Say, 'Jesus is Lord.'"

And every time Safia would begin to make this declaration, the demon within her would send her into great pain and cause her body to writhe. We would pray again, commanding the demon to leave her in the name of Jesus. I'm not sure how long we continued in this spiritual warfare, but then it happened. Once more, we commanded the demon to leave her, and this time her body not only grew quiet, but went completely limp. Suddenly, there was something different about her. She seemed to be at peace, maybe for the first time in years. Once more, I encouraged Safia to make a declaration of faith.

This time Safia opened her eyes and looked into mine, exclaiming, "Jesus is Lord!"

You might expect that we would break into celebration after such a prolonged struggle, but we didn't. We stood there in silence, knowing that Jesus had been in our midst. There was a holy hush that came upon those in Safia's room that day. Our hearts were thankful, and we stood in absolute awe of our Jesus. He had allowed us the holy privilege of being used by him as he set free this young woman who had been imprisoned by Satan for so long. And free she was.

This happened nearly ten years ago, and today Safia is still serving the Lord. The generational curse that enslaved the women of her family has been broken. Jesus had set her free. The demons tremble in fear before him.[2]

* * *

Legion was a man who lived centuries before Safia. He had a problem as well—an even a bigger problem than Safia's. He too was demon possessed, but the Bible tells us that he was filled with so many demons that he was given the name Legion. During his lifetime, Rome controlled much of the known world through formidable military force. A legion was a military unit comprised of 5,000 to 6,000 fighting men. This man who lived in Jesus' day was called Legion because there were so many demons within him. Were there 5,000-6,000? I don't know, but there were many.

He was so depraved that he lived in the tombs, with the dead as his companions. He would cry out from the cemetery night after night, shrieking in pain as he cut himself with stones. The villagers tried to restrict his movement by chaining his hands and feet, but he was so fierce that he would break the chains with ease. He would run naked and wild like an animal. If there were ever a worst-case scenario when it came to spiritual afflictions, this was it. He lived in pain and agony, completely under the devil's control until he met Jesus.[3]

The demons within Legion begged Jesus to allow them to go into a herd of pigs. Jesus gave his permission and the demons left the man, entering the pigs. (Don't miss the fact that the demons could not do anything in the presence of Jesus without his permission.) After the demons left the man and entered the pigs, the pigs ran down the hill and into the lake and drowned—all 2,000 of them.

Those tending the pigs ran off to tell the villagers what had happened to Legion and what had happened to the pigs. When they returned, they brought many of the villagers with them. And when they came to the place where the miracle had taken place, there was Legion, sitting quietly, fully dressed and in his right mind.

There is nothing that Jesus cannot do. No matter how far gone a person might be, there is no one beyond the help of Jesus—not Safia, not Legion, not anyone. Jesus is not even stopped by Satan and his demons. The enemy can't slow Jesus' mission of saving people and bringing them into the kingdom. In fact, that was Christ's promise: even "the gates of Hades will not overcome [the church]" (Matthew 16:18). Jesus is building his church and not even the demons in hell can stop him. The church is unstoppable!

8
PERSECUTION

"On that day a great persecution broke out against the church in Jerusalem, and all except the apostles were scattered. . . ."
—Acts 8:1

The day began like many other days. Jacob officiated at a funeral service in the morning. Funerals took so much of his time these days. Then a family called him to their home, concerned that someone in their village had given their daughter the "evil eye."[1] He counseled them in how to protect themselves from this curse, encouraging them to call upon Ariel, the angel of protection. Before he left, Jacob gave the daughter an amulet to wear. Many of his people wore amulets around their wrists to ward off evil. Tomorrow was the Sabbath, so he needed to work with the other priests to prepare for the Eucharist. As a priest, this was his most important duty.

As a boy, Jacob had always wanted to be a priest. When he was just seven years old, he left home to live with a priest and attend the religious school that prepared him to become a deacon. He was ordained as a deacon when he was fifteen and continued his religious training for the next four years. Finally, he was ready to apply for the priesthood. But before he could be ordained, he had to make a decision that would last a lifetime. He had to either commit himself to a life of celibacy or get married before the rite of ordination. He chose to get married.

As a priest who was married prior to his ordination, he would not be allowed to end his marriage. Divorce and remarriage or adultery resulted in a loss of purity, which would immediately terminate his ordination. Jacob, however, would never think of breaking his covenant with his wife. He loved her, as he did his two small children. He was thrilled with his station in life. This is all he had ever wanted to be: a priest fulfilling his call to serve God.

And yet, on this day as he left the home of the people who had requested his help in warding off the evil eye, he could not help but wonder if there was more. He had done well in his theological studies. He had gained a position of great influence in the community. He had a great family, and he was serving God. But God seemed so far away. All his training had done little to prepare him to know the God whom he served. As he thought on these things, he passed a small café where many were gathered for coffee and conversation. A young woman was coming out the door of the café. She greeted him, "Good afternoon, Your Holiness."

He crossed her face three times with a wooden cross, and she bowed to accept his blessing. It was then that he decided to stop for a cup of coffee. He sat at a small table and ordered his favorite pick-me-up. He liked his coffee strong, but with ample cream and several heaping spoons of sugar. He sipped at his drink as the room boomed with chatter. Everyone was engaged in vigorous conversation, but he sat all alone. It reminded him of his lack of intimacy with God.

"May I sit here?"

Roused from his deep meditation, he looked up and saw a young man standing before him. Although Jacob did not know the man, his priestly garb revealed him to be a colleague.

"Of course," Jacob replied. "Please join me."

When Jacob asked the young priest where he served, he stated that he was from a village in the far south of the country but was traveling in the north on personal business.

He introduced himself. "My name is Abraham."

As Abraham continued to talk, Jacob was amazed at the conversation. Abraham was talking about God like he knew him on a personal level. Somehow this young priest was able to disarm Jacob so he confessed that he did not have the close relationship with God that he wanted.

Jacob was shocked when Abraham began talking about Jesus. He had learned about Jesus in his theological training, but to call him "Jesus" was not something that was done. He was called by other names, like "Emmanuel" or "Redeemer," but never "Jesus." Abraham was dressed like a priest, but he talked like one of those evangelical Christians who were constantly trying to proselytize Jacob's people. They were always talking about Jesus. But no one from Jacob's religious group would use such language. In fact, Jacob and his people reacted violently to people who used that name. Once, when an evangelical was preaching about Jesus in their community, a man in the crowd grabbed the evangelical's tongue, pulling it from his mouth, as another took his knife and cut it off. That man never spoke the name of Jesus again.

There was another Christian evangelist who dared to speak about Jesus publicly. This time, the excited mob took an axe and chopped the man into small pieces. It was not humane, Jacob thought, but someone had to protect their faith from those heretics.

If Jacob were honest with himself, he would have to confess it was more about protecting the institution he served and preventing the loss of their long-standing traditions and rich culture. Either way,

Jacob was quite surprised that Abraham, a fellow priest, was talking so much about Jesus. He would have protested, but he couldn't help noticing the difference between Abraham's relationship with God and his own. He wanted to hear more from the young priest.

That was the day when everything changed for Jacob. He planned several more meetings with Abraham. It was not long before Jacob realized that Jesus was greater than Mary. He was loftier than the angels. He was greater than all the saints. Jacob came to know that Jesus demanded more than an intellectual faith. He had always believed that Jesus died on the cross to save the world from sin, but he had never realized that the world is saved one person at a time. All people in the world have to go to Jesus on their own, confess their sins, and repent from their sin.

Jacob knew that repentance meant he had to turn away from his old life of trusting in his good works and put his whole trust in what Jesus had done for him. In his mind's eye, he could almost see Jesus hanging on the cross. In that same moment, Jacob's life passed before his eyes. He could see his sins. He had been called "Your Holiness" by his people, but he saw that he was far from the righteousness of his God. He knew that all of his service to God had been self-serving. Jacob was far more interested in himself than he was focused on God. The realization crept into his consciousness that he loved himself more than God, and certainly more than he loved the people he served in his capacity as priest.

Jacob fell to his knees and confessed his sin to Jesus. He had never been as serious about anything before, as he was when he promised Jesus that he would live for him. Jacob trusted Jesus. He knew that Jesus had forgiven his every sin. That was the day that Jacob began a personal relationship with God, and Jesus became his Savior and his Lord.

In the days that followed, Jacob discovered that Abraham was more than a priest. Abraham held ordination papers within the same institution that Jacob served, but he also was an underground evangelist in the Church of the Nazarene. He was a priest reaching other priests for Jesus. Jacob's heart began to yearn to lead others to Jesus, and soon he became a Nazarene house church leader in the city where he lived.

He was trained to work with underground strategies. This meant that he would approach people privately. He would build relationships with those people until they came to a place of trust. Then he would proclaim to them the truth about Jesus. Those who believed in Jesus were invited to join the church that met in his home. His church was quiet about their worship. If they were discovered, heavy persecution would follow. Worse than that, they would no longer be effective in their evangelism efforts.

How could they lead people to Christ if they were avoided by the same people they tried to reach? No one would talk to evangelicals in his city. If they did, their friends and family would think that they had become evangelical Christians, and they would be persecuted. An underground approach was the most effective way to accomplish their mission in this gospel-resistant region of their country.

Then one day as Jacob prayed, God spoke to him. It was not a voice spoken aloud, but more like a strong impression that entered his mind. He knew it was the voice of God. He had become accustomed to hearing the still, small voice of God within him.

The Lord told him, *Do not continue to speak about me in this underground way. I want you to preach about me on the street. Tell people publicly who I am and what I have done for you.*

Jacob obeyed. Immediately, he went to the streets and preached about Jesus to all who passed by. People were greatly disturbed by this new, strange teaching. Once the priests in the community were informed, they filed false charges against Jacob with the authorities. Jacob was arrested and thrown into jail. He found eight other Christians from evangelical denominations in jail with him. They too had been arrested under false accusations after speaking of Jesus publicly.

Not many days had passed when a policeman opened their cell doors and ordered them to move out. The officer took the nine men to the city square where community meetings were held, then forced them to stand in a line facing the entire community. Six thousand people had shown up to wait for the judgment of the nine evangelicals who dared to preach about Jesus publicly. As they were lined up, a number of the priests from the city approached them.

They commanded the prisoners, "You will deny Jesus today before your community. You have spoken his name publicly, so now you will publicly deny him. If you do not, you will be beaten and put back in jail. You may even die today."

The prisoners were forced to step forward one at a time. The first prisoner stepped forward and denied Jesus. Then the second did the same. They did so out of fear. Each one publicly denied Jesus until it was Jacob's turn. Jacob stepped forward and saw his wife and small children in the crowd. They wondered what their husband and father would do.

Jacob stepped out and declared in a strong voice, "I will never deny Jesus. You can beat me. You can put me in prison. You can even kill me. But I will never deny Jesus. He is my Lord and my Savior. I will follow him the rest of my life."

The priests were infuriated. They rushed up to Jacob and began to beat him with their prayer sticks.

He was struck in the head, then up and down his body with many blows, until a cry came from the crowd.

Someone yelled out, "Stop that! Do not beat Jacob like this."

Someone else in the crowd yelled at the priests, "We know this man. Jacob lives a better life than any of us do. He even lives a better life than you, our religious leaders."

Miraculously, the whole crowd began to plead in unison for Jacob's life. Most crowds in that region would cut off the tongues of people who spoke about Jesus or, if necessary, chop them into pieces to silence them. But on this day, they turned against their religious leaders to intercede for Jacob, the man who dared to speak the name of Jesus.

The priests stopped beating Jacob because of the pressure from the crowd. And then, one of the eight who had denied Jesus stepped forward and pleaded with the crowd.

"Wait! Please hear me. I sinned against God when I denied Jesus. I did so out of fear. But I repent from this sin right now. I will never deny him again."

Then a second man stepped forward and confessed his sin, and then another, and another, until five of the eight men repented of denying Jesus.

One of the evangelicals who repented that day said, "We like what we see in this man, Jacob. We are going to join him, and together we are going to share

Jesus with all of you until this whole city knows the truth about Jesus. Then we will move on to the surrounding villages and preach Jesus to them."

A miracle has taken place in this city. In a community that once cut off the tongues of those who uttered the name of Jesus, Christ's name is now on every tongue. The men discuss Jesus in the coffee shops; the women talk about him as they wash clothes at the river; and even the children speak Jesus' name in their schools. The conversation throughout the city is about Jesus.

The people in that community often ask, "Have our priests told us the truth about Jesus all of these years, or is it Jacob who speaks the truth?"

Many in this city have come to Christ already, but many more will follow. A determined team of evangelicals who work with Jacob are today reaching not only Jacob's city, but also villages throughout that region of the country. Persecution resulted in disciples being scattered throughout the country with a new boldness to reach their world for Christ.

Persecution has never been effective in stopping the spread of the gospel. From the beginning of the church's history, persecution has worked to the benefit of the church. In the book of Acts, we learn of a great persecution that broke out against the Christians. Stephen was stoned to death in the streets. Other Christians were hunted down and beaten or murdered. The disciples began to scatter.[2] All except the apostles fled from Jerusalem. They fled to the countryside. They fled to the cities, not only in Israel but also in territories beyond. And everywhere these Christians went, they told people the good news of Jesus, and Christianity spread.

The church thrives when persecuted. There is nothing that can stop Jesus from building his church. The more the enemy raises his ugly head, the more the church grows. Without a doubt, the church is unstoppable!

9
MARTYRS

"The blood of the martyrs is the seed of the church."
—Tertullian, 2nd-century church father

Tamim was a Sufi Muslim in a country with a predominantly Sunni population. As a Sufi, Tamim believed that he could draw closer to God and that his inner character would become purer through his experience with the divine. The vast majority of young men in his country cared little about inner transformation. In fact, many men his age were addicted to drugs and alcohol and wasted their days pursuing their addictions. Many were jobless. They supported their habits by either living off their relatives or by seeking money through various illegal activities. Crime was rampant in his country.

Tamim was a bright light in a very dark world. He was a clean, hardworking man who never smoked and would not touch alcohol. He refused to chase after women like so many of his friends did. He was an industrious young man. He lived in a city with a population of nearly one million, where finding employment was a huge challenge. Tamim, however, was always able to find a job, though some of his jobs came without a salary. A generous man, he also gave to the needy. He shared whatever he had with his fellow man. Even at the young age of twenty-two, he had gained the respect of everyone in his community. His hair was not gray; nevertheless, he was viewed as an "elder" in his community.

He then met a man named Sahib, who would later become one of his best friends. Sahib had recently moved to the city where Tamim lived because his wife needed medical attention that was not available in the small town where they had lived most of their lives.

From their first meeting, Tamim was drawn to Sahib. There was something about him. It was not just that Sahib was a moral person like him. True, Sahib did not drink, smoke, or waste his days away like so many others. And he treated his wife with such respect. Tamim could easily see that Sahib loved his family deeply. But there was something else about Sahib that Tamim could not quite pinpoint.

As the days passed, Sahib began to open up to Tamim. He referenced the Qur'an often. He talked about the prophets starting with Adam, but it was the prophet Jesus on whom Sahib focused. It was Sahib's question that first grabbed Tamim by the heart and wouldn't let him go.

"Who was the purest of all the prophets?" Sahib asked.

After a little thought, Tamim had to admit that it was Jesus. The Qur'an proclaimed that Jesus had lived a "sinless" life. No one else had ever accomplished such a feat. Tamim began to study all of the references to Jesus in the Qur'an and often discussed his findings with his new friend.

One day Sahib said to Tamim, "Why don't you study the Gospels? There is much more about this Jesus revealed in those Holy Scriptures."

Tamim thought that would be proper since the Qur'an encouraged Muslims to read the Gospels. After all, the Qur'an proclaimed that the Gospels were revealed by God. Even so, it felt strange to open a Bible and turn to the Gospels. The Qur'an may have granted permission, but his Muslim community would certainly oppose it. His Islamic friends said that the Gospels had been corrupted by the Christians and that the reliability of the Gospels found in the Christians' Bible could not be trusted. That had never made sense to Tamim.

He thought, *How could that be? First, the Qur'an speaks of the Gospels as the revealed Word of God. Second, the Qur'an states that God protects his Word by making it incorruptible. But then, Muslims proclaim that Christians have corrupted the Gospels.*

Tamim was not a college graduate, but he knew there was something wrong with the logic that would lead to such a conclusion. Tamim hoped that as he read through the Gospels, the dilemma would be resolved. His only purpose was to find out more about the prophet Jesus and what had enabled him to live a perfect life. Certainly, if he had never sinned, his life was just that—a perfect one. He had not read very far when one of Jesus' statements caught his attention: "Blessed are the pure in heart, for they will see God."[1]

The statement burned within Tamim as he read it. His character could improve, but could it become perfect? Could he attain purity of heart in this life? That was the first question he asked Sahib when he saw him the following day. Sahib just smiled and remarked that Jesus was gaining another disciple.

Day after day, Tamim studied the Gospels. Day after day, he had questions for Sahib. Then one day, Sahib confessed that he was a disciple of Jesus. He told Tamim that there were others in their city who were following Jesus as well.

Then Sahib invited Tamim to attend a meeting at an underground house church. The invitation was not given lightly. The members of this house church were already watching Tamim closely. Though Tamim had no idea that he was being watched, they observed everything he did and examined everything he said. The members of the house church were looking for clues as to whether Tamim was a true seeker. Sometimes people who identified themselves as seekers of Jesus turned out to be plants trying to identify the locations of house churches. If the members were betrayed, the house church would be extinguished. They would each be hunted down and killed. However, the people of Sahib's house church believed that Tamim was a genuine seeker, and they voted unanimously for Sahib to extend the invitation to him.

When Friday came, Tamim came to the house where the church met. But he could not walk into the house with Sahib—he had been given specific instructions to walk to the house alone. He had also been instructed to leave alone. They could not call any attention to the house. When Tamim entered, the church members were sitting on cushions on the floor with windows closed and doors locked. They sang their songs in a chant, as though they were reading from the Qur'an. They sang quietly so that no one outside the home could hear them.

Quiet as it was, there was an inexpressible joy that flooded the room. Tamim had never felt so close to God. It was what he had always sought as a Sufi—a closeness to his creator.

Then the members opened their Bibles and the leader began reading from John chapter 3. It was a story about a man named Nicodemus, a religious leader in that day. Nicodemus had approached Jesus just as Tamim had approached the house church—secretly, without being seen. Nicodemus came at night so that others would not see him associate with Jesus. Jesus was not impressed by Nicodemus' religious credentials, and told him that he would never enter the kingdom of God unless he was born again.

Tamim could understand Nicodemus' confusion with this teaching he received from Jesus. How could anyone be born again? But the leader explained that Jesus was telling Nicodemus he must be spiritually reborn. He was born physically into the world, but to enter the kingdom of God, he had to be born from above. God had to give him new life.

The house church came alive during this discussion. People joined in, giving testimony of how they had been born again when they turned away from their sin and self-righteousness and put their faith in Christ. The leader pointed out that this was exactly what Jesus was trying to tell Nicodemus. The leader then talked about the cross and how Jesus died to take away the sins of humanity. Tamim felt as though truth were rushing into his brain like an overflowing river. He could hardly digest it all in one sitting. He went away from the house church that first Friday with his mind swimming in a flood of new ideas, ideas that felt right, but couldn't be swallowed all at once. Tamim never missed a meeting after that. Soon, he gave his testimony of how he was trusting Jesus, and how he had found more intimacy with God that he ever could have hoped for. Tamim became a born-again Christian that year, when he was still twenty-two years old.

After that, Tamim cared even more deeply for others than he had before his encounter with Jesus Christ. He wanted to serve his community in the best way he could. He joined a local humanitarian organization and gave his life to meeting the needs of those who lived in his city. It was as if Jesus had given him a new love for people, even greater than he possessed before. And of first importance in his newfound passion for others was his desire to see them come to Christ and experience the same love for his Savior that he had. He reasoned that if he was compassionate in helping others with their physical needs, they would be more open to his message that Jesus was indeed more than a prophet—he was God himself who gave up his life by dying on the cross to take away the sins of the world.

Tamim had to be very careful, however, in how he approached people. He knew that he had to be as "shrewd as [a snake] and as innocent as [a dove]."[2] Jesus had warned his disciples that this kind of an approach was necessary in some situations. Even so, Tamim exposed himself to danger many times as he shared Jesus with his friends and other members of the community.

Soon, it became widely known that Tamim was a follower of Jesus. In his culture, he was seen as an unbeliever. It was for that reason that some men stopped his car one day, just three years after Tamim had met Jesus. They wore masks over their faces and dragged him before the villagers in a nearby community.

"Tamim," they said, "you have shamed your family and clan. Turn back to Islam now. If you do not, we will kill you today."

Tamim remained silent, ignoring the repeated warnings that he would die if he did not recant Christianity and return to Islam. One of the men recorded the scene with the video camera on his cell phone and another masked man read from the Qur'an. Again and again, Tamim was given opportunity to save his life.

"Just repent from your sin and return to Islam," they said.

Peace came over him. He wanted to live, but he was not afraid to die. Maybe he was thinking of the words he had read three years earlier: "Blessed are the pure in heart, for they will see God."[3] He knew that Jesus would not forsake him. The men pushed Tamim to his knees, and the one who held onto him stroked the back of a knife across the top of his head. It was the final warning.

"Tamim, just say the word. Confess your apostasy and turn back to Islam, and you will live."

Tamim's lips moved ever so slightly. Though no one knew for sure what he was saying, his Christian friends knew that he was praying.

"Father, forgive them. They do not know what they are doing."

Then the blade of the knife was pressed against his neck, and his persecutor began to cut off his head. Blood gushed throughout his slow death. Tamim's face revealed excruciating pain, but he never said a word. He never begged for mercy. He did not speak a word. He was beheaded for the sake of Jesus.

In the same breath that Jesus promised that the pure in heart would see God, he declared this: "Blessed are those who are persecuted because of righteousness, for theirs is the kingdom of heaven."[4]

The villagers who saw Tamim's death were not the only witnesses to this tragedy. The video Tamim's persecutors took that day was made into a DVD and circulated throughout the country. Eventually, the video found its way to the internet. It was a warning to every Muslim in that country that turning away from Islam would result in this kind of suffering. These radical, masked Muslims believed that the circulation of the video would end any advance of Christianity in their country, but they were dead wrong. Those who saw Tamim die that day could not believe that anyone would die as he did for a lie. Hearts were opened, and people began to trust in Jesus. Tamim's blood caused many to turn from Islam to Jesus.

Tamim is one of many who have died for Jesus in his country. The Church of the Nazarene conducted a study of the first eight years that the denomination began making disciples in this country, and discovered that fifteen Nazarenes had been slaughtered for their faith during those first eight years. Since that time, many more have died for Jesus. In fact, persecution has heightened in the succeeding years with an increased number of beheadings and other killings. In every case, an explosion of new converts has taken place in the vicinity of the martyrdom. In fact, in all fifteen locations where our people died for Christ, there are now clusters of underground house churches within a one-kilometer radius of the blood-stained ground.

Tertullian, one of our early church fathers, proclaimed that the "blood of the martyrs is the seed of the church." The more the enemy raises his ugly head against the church, the more Jesus carries out his promise: "I will build my church, and the gates of Hades will not overcome it" (Matthew 16:18). Not even persecution that leads to martyrdom can stop his church. The church is unstoppable!

10

TESTIMONY OF THE CRUCIFIED

"On this rock I will build my church . . ."
—Matthew 16:18

"Whoever wants to be my disciple must deny themselves and take up their cross and follow me."
—Matthew 16:24

The question did not surprise Peter. He had been thinking about it often. For almost three years now, he had watched Jesus do some amazing things. Jesus had cleansed the lepers, healed the blind, and made the deaf hear. The demon possessed were set free at his command. He had even raised the dead. He fed the multitudes with a portion of food that hardly would have satisfied Peter and his eleven friends. Shortly after that miracle, Peter saw Jesus walking on water. Peter believed that he too could walk on water if Jesus gave the invitation. And indeed, Peter had succeeded in doing so until he took his eyes off Jesus and focused instead on the wind and waves hurling about him.

The question was constantly before him: "Who is this man Jesus?"

So when Jesus asked, "Who do people say that I am?" on that day in Caesarea Philippi, Peter was not at all surprised by the question.

But he was surprised at the answer that came from his own mouth. "You are the Messiah, the Son of the living God."[1] Once he said it, he wondered where the words had come from.

Jesus answered that question. It was a truth revealed to him by the Father in heaven. And then Jesus made a spectacular promise that would give Peter encouragement for the rest of his life.

Jesus declared, "On this rock I will build my church, and the gates of Hades will not overcome it."[2]

Peter knew intuitively that Jesus meant it was on his declaration of faith—the declaration that Jesus was the Christ, the Anointed One, the Messiah—that Jesus would build his church. Peter would later come to understand that Jesus was talking not only about Peter's own testimony, but also about the testimony of all his disciples.

Peter felt good about himself. He had stumbled upon God's plan for how Jesus would build the church before any of the other disciples had. But his self-satisfaction did not last long. Soon afterward, Peter thoughtlessly chastised Jesus for predicting his own death in Jerusalem. How could it be that Jesus would be taken from them?

"Never, Lord!"[3] was his quick reaction to the terrible thought. How embarrassing it was to be put down so strongly in front of the other eleven. "Get behind me, Satan!"[4] Jesus rebuked him. So much for appearing spiritual before his friends!

It was then that Jesus' discussion transitioned from his impending death to the death of his disciples, saying, "Whoever wants to be my disciple must deny themselves and take up their cross and follow me."[5]

Peter often thought that he had denied himself many things to follow Jesus. After all, he had left his father and his fishing business behind. He did not know what else he could give up to become a disciple of Jesus. It was the mention of the cross that most confused him. What did Jesus mean when he said they must follow him to the cross?

It would not be until after Jesus' crucifixion that this question was answered. Suddenly, it made perfect sense. Peter came to realize that he himself would have to die. The Romans had made the cross a symbol of death. Peter remembered the awful day when he saw Jesus struggling through the streets, bearing the heavy, cruel cross upon his shoulders. He knew that Jesus' earlier words were about to come true: Jesus would die in Jerusalem, just as he had predicted in Caesarea Philippi. The cross told that story with perfect clarity. And Jesus told Peter to submit to this same cross.

Indeed, years later, Peter would end up dying on a cross. He would insist that he be nailed upside down, because he was not worthy to die like his Savior. This, however, was not the cross Jesus was speaking about. It was a completely different kind of death to which Jesus was calling his disciples. He did not understand any of this on that day in Caesarea Philippi.

It was not until those ten days when he and the other disciples waited in the upper room for the gift the Father had promised that he began to search his own soul. He confessed to the other disciples that he had denied Christ three times while he sat in the courtyard waiting to find out what would happen to Jesus.[6]

During those days in the upper room, Peter began to understand that there was a self-centeredness within him that caused him to struggle in his witness for Christ. Jesus had been very clear that his plan was to build the church through the testimony of his disciples. And now, as he waited in the upper room, it finally dawned on Peter that through the testimony of Jesus' disciples, Jesus would powerfully impact the world.

For Peter, those ten days were days of confessing to the church and to the Lord, and of dying to himself. When Jesus spoke of sacrifice, he meant more than denying oneself of home, family, and business. It had finally become clear to Peter that he had to die to his every desire—his hopes, goals, and future.

Paul declared his testimony when he said, "I have been crucified with Christ and I no longer live, but Christ lives in me. The life I now live in the body, I live by faith in the Son of God, who loved me and gave himself for me."[7]

Peter finally understood that Jesus' plan for building his church was to use the testimonies of the crucified[8]—testimonies about who Jesus is and what he has done.

Consider where you are today. Have you confessed your sins and trusted in Jesus, who died to take away those sins? If not, Christ invites you to enter into a relationship with him. To do so, you can pray this simple prayer:

Jesus, forgive me for my sins. I now turn away from those sins and away from my life without you. I believe in my heart that you, Jesus, died for me and have taken those sins away. Thank you for eternal life. Amen.

If you have been following Jesus, consider now who is in control of your life. Have you died to yourself? Have you given your life completely to God? Just as Peter was completely changed by his experience in the upper room,[9] you too can be radically transformed by dying to yourself and consecrating your life entirely to God. This radical transformation can be experienced by praying this simple prayer:

Thank you, Jesus, for saving me from my sins and adopting me into your family. As a child of God, I now give you my life completely. I freely choose to die to myself. Fill me with your spirit, cleanse my self-centered nature, and take absolute control of my life.

If you sincerely prayed that prayer, trusting Jesus to cleanse the inner nature and fill you with his spirit, he will empower you to witness for him.

Jesus will use you to build his church through your testimony that he is the Christ, the one set apart from all eternity to save his people from their sins.

Jesus will build his church. He will do it through those who are willing to die to self and testify of who Jesus is and what he has done for them. Where the crucified testify about their wonderful Jesus, the church is truly unstoppable!

NOTES

Chapter 2

1. The Injeel is the Arabic name for what Muslims believe to be the original Gospel of Jesus.

2. Underground Christians are those who do not make their faith in Christ known publicly for security reasons. They share their faith privately with individuals whom they trust to hold their conversations confidential.

3. God has accepted those martyrs into his glorious kingdom of heaven. They were faithful to Jesus Christ and to his testimony until the end. As Jesus said in Revelation 2:10, "Be faithful, even to the point of death, and I will give you life as your victor's crown." May God grant that those murderers will come to see that Jesus Christ is Lord. May they ask Jesus Christ to forgive them of their sins.

4. 1 Peter 5:8

Chapter 3

1. John 14:6

2. Ephesians 2:8-9

3. Mark 1:15

4. Kevin Greeson, *The Camel* (Arkadelphia, AR: WIGTake Resources, 2007), 50.

5. The reader can refer to pages 50 and 51 of Greeson's book for additional stories of Muslims coming to Christ through dreams.

Chapter 4

1. Chat causes an unreasonable optimism among those who chew it.

2. 2 Corinthians 5:17

3. 10-40 Window is a term that represents the geographical area in the Eastern Hemisphere, plus the European and African part of the Western Hemisphere, located between 10 and 40 degrees north of the equator. This region of the world has the least access to the Christian message and Christian resources.

4. Exodus, chapters 5 through 14.

Chapter 5

1. Animism is the worldview of those who do not acknowledge a Creator and instead worship creation.

2. Most people in southern Sudan owned AK-47s to protect their families from thieves who would rustle their cattle, from the threats of tribal warfare, and from a long-standing war with the North.

3. Mark 4:41

Chapter 6

1. Shahada is the Islamic creed proclaimed in the Muslim's daily prayers that "there is only one God, Allah, and Muhammad is his prophet."

2. Obligatory ritual fasting in the month of Ramadan

3. Almsgiving

4. Salat consists of five daily prayers performed in a specific ritualistic manner.

5. Pilgrimage to the holy city Mecca that every Muslim should make at least once in his lifetime

6. Arabic for infidels

7. Acts 3

Chapter 7

1. Demonic possession has been denied by much of the western world, but a quick read through the New Testament will supply much biblical evidence of its existence. I have personally witnessed many demons being cast out of people both in the East and West.

2. James 2:19

3. Mark chapter 5

Chapter 8

1. The "evil eye" is a look of envy or dislike that is believed by many cultures to cause injury or bad luck for the person at whom it is directed.

2. Acts 8:1

Chapter 9

1. Matthew 5:8
2. Matthew 10:16
3. Matthew 5:8
4. Matthew 5:10

Chapter 10

1. Matthew 16:16
2. Matthew 16:18
3. Matthew 16:22
4. Matthew 16:23
5. Matthew 16:24
6. Matthew 26:69-75
7. Galatians 2:20
8. Those who respond to the urging of the apostle Paul in Romans 12:1 to "offer [their] bodies as living sacrifice[s]."
9. See the Book of Acts, chapters 1 through 4.